THE GARDENS
AT FILOLI

THE GARDENS
AT FILOLI

PHOTOGRAPHS BY *Christopher McMahon*

TEXT BY *Timmy Gallagher*

POMEGRANATE ARTBOOKS

San Francisco

Photograph on title page: View of the Sundial through Filoli Gate.

Published by Pomegranate Artbooks
Box 6099, Rohnert Park, California 94927
Pomegranate Catalog No. A743

Library of Congress Cataloging-in-Publication Data

McMahon, Christopher.
    The gardens at Filoli / photographs by Christopher McMahon ; text by Timmy Gallagher. —
1st ed.

        p.   cm.
    ISBN 1-56640-993-4
    1. Filoli Gardens (Calif.) 2. Filoli Gardens (Calif.)—Pictorial works. I. Gallagher, Timmy. II. Title.
    SB466.U7F545 1994
    712'.5'097946—dc20   94-17778
                                                                                                        CIP

Designed by Bonnie Smetts Design

06 05 04 03 02 01 00 99 98 97   11 10 9 8 7 6 5 4 3

To my wife, Suzanne;

my mother, Betty Longshore;

and all my co-workers at Filoli

— C. M.

CONTENTS

PHOTOGRAPHER'S PREFACE

I first heard of the Filoli estate in Woodside, California, in 1984, when I was seeking to advance my career in the horticultural field. Until then my gardening experience had included working in the tomato fields in Chico, California; participating in the life of a farming community in India for three years; co-owning a lawn service business; maintaining the grounds of a couple of large apartment complexes; developing the ornamental-agricultural landscape in an innovative planned community (the last three projects were in Davis, California); and operating a fresh and dried cut flower business with my mother in the Sierra Nevada. The broad range of these activities and the horticultural skills I developed during them were an excellent preparation for entering the refined world of estate gardening at Filoli.

It is difficult to describe the personal impact of my first visit to the estate. It was like entering a world I had no idea existed. I had no conception that a world-class garden equivalent in almost every respect to the grand estates of Europe, particularly England, existed right in the Bay Area, thirty miles south of San Francisco. As I walked through the garden with my wife on the day of my job interview, one immaculately maintained area after another appeared before my enchanted eyes. My heart was filled with a deep longing to participate in the gardening activities of such a refined environment. Fortunately, that desire was fulfilled. In May I embarked on my career as an estate gardener in one of the most beautiful formal display gardens in the United States.

One of the most significant professional developments that occurs when one works in such an environment is the emergence of a sense of being a craftsperson and artist. A great garden is an ever-changing three-dimensional work of art that requires constant maintenance to keep it looking pristine and immaculate. In the beginning of such an apprenticeship, one hardly has time to think about anything but getting the basic tasks done—mowing, blowing, edging, weeding, planting, fertilizing, pruning and the like—but it is in doing these jobs well and thoroughly that a sense of refinement begins to develop and one begins to realize how every aspect of the work helps create the innumerable visions of beauty such an estate possesses. In such an environment one derives joy not only from developing horticultural skills and knowledge but also from being part of a guild of professional gardeners who each possess unique talents and perceptions that enhance one's own. It has been my greatest good fortune to have worked with some of the finest horticulturists I have ever known; association with them has made my life richer in many ways far beyond horticultural concerns. Indeed, the beauty depicted in these pages is a tribute to the warmth, kindness and friendship my co-workers and I enjoyed while working to share the garden's loveliness with others.

It was about seven years before I was sufficiently acquainted with the garden's seasonal routines to begin to appreciate many of the subtler aspects of the beauty I was involved with creating. This was a critical juncture because at that point I had participated in almost every horticultural activity on the grounds numerous times and had begun to fall into the familiarity of those routines almost unthinkingly. Fortunately, at that time a desire came to develop some new skill that would allow me to capture visually the beauty of the garden through the seasons, so I decided to take up photography. Even had this project merely reawakened my sense of wonder and awe toward the beauty of nature in general and of gardens specifically, it would have been well worth it. As it turned out, however, friends, co-workers and associates of the estate became interested in what I was doing and the idea arose to offer to the public a collection of images of the estate through the seasons of the year.

The results are found in the pages of this book. Thousands of photographs were taken and hundreds of hours were spent in the garden in the early hours before work and on weekends trying to capture some of the magic of Filoli. Even so, it is possible to depict only a tiny reflection of those precious, transcendent moments when the heart is touched in ways no word or image can describe. Still, I hope these vignettes of beauty will invoke for others some of what we have felt while working in the garden.

I also hope this book will encourage others to explore the gardens in their own vicinities and to do what they can to support those gardens' exis-

OPPOSITE: View of Filoli through oak branches on a hill overlooking the estate, facing west

tence. In our area, Filoli is one of the last great estates with house and garden intact from a golden era of San Francisco's history when numerous such estates flourished, so the benefit of preserving such sanctuaries of beauty has been before me almost every day I have worked on the estate. I have watched our 60,000 yearly guests arrive at the garden's entrance burdened with cares and worries and leave refreshed, a vision of beauty and delight imprinted on their hearts. A well-maintained garden, be it great or small, keeps us in contact with the natural world and inspires us to keep our hearts and minds open to positive, sublime influences that can enrich our lives immeasurably. It would benefit us to envision our gardens as true national treasures so they may be preserved and maintained for future generations.

AUTHOR'S PREFACE

Filoli is a remarkably beautiful 654-acre historic estate set in a wooded valley about thirty miles south of San Francisco. In 1915 the estate's first owner, William Bowers Bourn II, commissioned prominent San Francisco architect Willis Polk to build Filoli's brick mansion, and the Bourns took up residence there in 1917. Bourn extracted the name for his estate from the words of a credo he admired: "Fight for a just cause, love your fellow man, live a good life."

Bourn's friend Bruce Porter designed Filoli's elegant formal gardens, and Bella Worn supervised their planting. The gardens' initial design and plant choices were maintained by the William P. Roths, the second owners of the estate. Today, as part of the National Trust for Historic Preservation, Filoli continues to showcase world-renowned gardens reminiscent of the finest European manors.

Surrounded by native oak woodlands, Filoli extends west to the Coast Range mountains; to the east, north and south, its magnificent views are protected by watershed property owned by the city of San Francisco. From Cañada Road, one enters Filoli through a simple wire gate framed by two pollarded London plane trees behind a chain link fence. A modest wooden sign says simply "Filoli." On either side of the road stand ancient deciduous California valley oaks (*Quercus lobata*). These stately trees are the monarchs of the western deciduous oaks, with their magnificent crowns and their low, sweeping branches that provide generous expanses of shade. The fields surrounding the estate are planted in oat hay, which is cut and baled before the dry season begins. California black-tailed deer browse among the young shoots, as do Canada geese, which arrive in November and leave in April. The handsome California quail, sporting a forward-curving black plume atop its head, gleans the oats that fall from the hay.

To the north, past the hay fields and oak woodlands, stately blue Atlas cedars (*Cedrus atlantica* 'Glauca') announce the beginning of the landscaped gardens. In their almost seventy years at Filoli, these enormous trees have grown much faster than they would have in their native habitat, Morocco's Atlas Mountains. Most of the original native evergreen oak trees, the coast live oaks (*Quercus agrifolia*), remain at Filoli today. These trees are hundreds of years old, and they receive excellent care to ensure that they will grace the landscape for centuries to come. In addition, a specimen of deciduous native oak (*Quercus lobata*) still stands inside the gardens, near the Garden Pavilion. Numerous Irish yews (*Taxus baccata* 'Stricta') throughout the gardens tie the various landscape areas together and, in some areas, provide a strong architectural feature. Pleached and pollarded London plane trees (*Platanus* x *acerifolia*) line the high brick wall that extends from the Walled Garden's main gate to the former Tennis Court dressing rooms. Between their trunks, various species of ivy (*Hedera* sp.) are kept neatly pruned within designated spaces on the wall to create a lush green tapestry effect.

In beds along the north side of the garden, original plantings of New Zealand tea trees (*Leptospermum scoparium* cultivars) have acquired in age a shaggy bark that hangs in ribbons from their branches. One variety, *L. scoparium* 'Nicholsii', seldom seen in gardens today, caused great excitement at the Chelsea Flower Show in 1912, where it won a medal for the most outstanding shrub to be introduced. Crossing of this rare red-flowered variety with white-flowered species has produced many of the spectacular varieties used today, several of which are featured at Filoli.

Filoli's gardens were photographed extensively by the estate's previous two owners, so a complete photographic record exists of the initial plantings. This has been a great help in keeping the original trees and shrubs within the garden's initial design. For example, at one point the Irish yews were outgrowing the gardens and had to be severely pruned back, as did the yew hedge (*Taxus* x *media*) in the Sunken Garden and the Grecian laurel shrubs (*Laurus nobilis*) in the Walled Garden.

The Filoli estate has twenty-seven acres of formal landscaped area, most of it separated from the surrounding terrain by a low brick wall. Of this area, sixteen acres are occupied by the gardens. The most abundant plants in the gardens are roses and camellias—the 650 rose plants represent more than 375 different varieties, 185 of which are various hybrid tea roses, producing an abundance of bloom from May through October. The 368 camellia bushes include 8 species and 127 varieties. Roses and camellias are added to the gardens on a continual basis. Other important plant collections feature Japanese maples, peonies and magnolias. Charming brick paths and wooden benches invite visitors to linger in the various gardens, from the intricate Knot Gardens to the romantic Wedding Place to the Chartres Cathedral Window Garden, reminiscent of the windows of the French cathedral. Seasonal color and fragrance abound throughout the gardens in an ever-changing array of annual and perennial plantings. All are arranged around Filoli's focal point, a sundial inscribed with the words "Time Began in a Garden."

Docent-led tours are offered of both house and gardens, and, on certain days, self-guided tours are permitted.* Docent-led nature tours are also conducted in the beautiful and historic undeveloped back property of Filoli. Trails lead past a former Ohlone Indian village site and the San Andreas fault and through second-growth redwoods (*Sequoia sempervirens*), oak and mixed evergreen forest, chaparral areas and virgin fir forest. A picturesque creek flanked with native ferns runs down from the mountains over moss-covered rocks and into an earthen reservoir. After heavy winter storms, the reservoir's overflow flume becomes a noisy, rushing waterfall flowing down to join the creek below the dam. An important educational attraction, Filoli's back country is popular with schoolchildren and hiking and natural history enthusiasts.

Whether the visitor to Filoli chooses a stroll through the mansion and elegantly landscaped formal gardens or a hike in the historic surrounding countryside, there is much to be seen and enjoyed in this grand estate at any time of year.

*After the first week in November, Filoli is closed to visitors as preparations are made for "Christmas at Filoli." During the first week of December, each year the mansion is decorated with a different holiday theme, entertainment is provided and plants, gifts and books are offered for sale. Filoli then closes for the winter, reopening in mid-February.

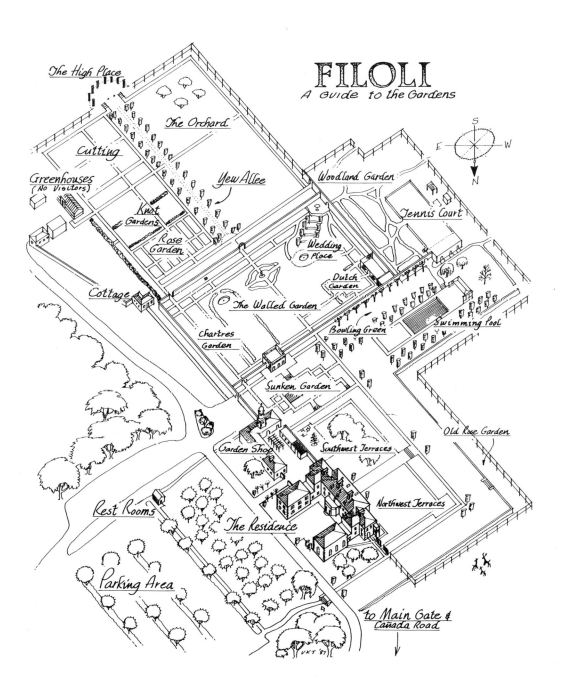

FILOLI
A Guide to the Gardens

The High Place

The Orchard

Cutting

Greenhouses
(No Visitors)

Yew Allee

Woodland Garden

Tennis Court

Knot Gardens

Rose Garden

Wedding Place

Dutch Garden

Cottage

The Walled Garden

Swimming Pool

Chartres Garden

Bowling Green

Sunken Garden

Old Rose Garden

Garden Shop

Southwest Terraces

Rest Rooms

Northwest Terraces

The Residence

Parking Area

to Main Gate &
Cañada Road

VKT '87

THE BUILDING OF FILOLI

Mr. and Mrs. William Bowers Bourn II

Filoli, located in a beautiful oak-studded valley on the eastern side of California's Coast Range, is the only one of the San Francisco Bay Area's great mansions and gardens to survive with its original view and setting, protected by the watershed property of San Francisco to the north, south and east. To the west the Filoli estate extends to the top ridge of the mountains, encompassing 654 acres.

William Bowers Bourn II, the builder of Filoli, loved the valley, with its view of Crystal Springs Lake to the north and the wooded coastal mountains to the west. The house and gardens were carefully placed to capture the beauty of the natural landscape. Only in recent years has the lake view been obscured by growth of the oak trees on the watershed property. Bourn owned the Spring Valley Water Company, which controlled the watershed lands and supplied water to the city of San Francisco, so the view was preserved during his lifetime: he could prune out oak branches or trees that might obstruct the view. In the 1930s, Bourn sold his company to the city of San Francisco.

Bourn's father came from Yonkers, New York, to San Francisco as a wealthy merchant in 1850 to join his business partner and father-in-law, Captain George Chase, with whom he owned a half interest in sailing ships. After setting up their shipping business, the senior Bourn purchased real estate in San Francisco and bought a partnership in a hard rock gold mine, the Empire Mine in Grass Valley. He later bought control of the mine, which under new management became the chief source of the Bourn family's wealth. In 1854 Bourn's wife joined him.

William Bowers Bourn II was born in 1857 and grew up in the family home on top of Nob Hill, at 1105 Taylor Street. When he was fifteen he began spending most of his time at the family's summer home and vineyard in St. Helena, known as Madroño. Two years later, in 1874, his father died suddenly, and the following year Bourn was sent to England to attend Cambridge University. While at Cambridge he had the opportunity to see the great houses and gardens of England. During his fourth year there a crisis occurred at the Empire Mine: it bottomed at the 1,200-foot level, with all visible ore exhausted. Bourn had to return to California to take over management of the mine and the vineyards at Madroño.

Bourn pursued further exploration of the mine, and after three years an even richer gold vein was discovered. In 1881, with his continued wealth ensured, Bourn married Agnes Moody of Yonkers. The following year a son was born, who died in infancy, and a year later, a daughter, Maud.

In 1888–1889 Bourn built the great Greystone Winery in St. Helena, the largest stone winery in the world. The building still stands, but today it is used by the Culinary Institute of America and houses classes for culinary professionals.

In 1890 Bourn became president of the San Francisco Gas Company and asked his longtime friend and hunting companion Willis Polk to design a home for him at 2550 Webster Street—on the hill above the gas company— and a summer home at the Empire Mine in Grass Valley. Polk was a very creative and imaginative architect. He designed most of the buildings rebuilt after the fire that followed the 1906 earthquake in San Francisco, and he was chairman of the architectural committee for the 1915 Panama Pacific International Exposition in San Francisco, which celebrated the opening of the Panama Canal. For Bourn's house on Webster Street Polk used clinker brick, brick that has been burned in the kiln. It had been the least expensive brick available until Bourn's house was made of it, and then it became fashionable and was in great demand. The buildings at the mine were made of quartz rock from the mine and trimmed in brick.

After the earthquake and fire, many of San Francisco's wealthy families did not rebuild their homes. Instead they moved to the peninsula south of San Francisco and built large, expensive estates. The San Jose–San Francisco Railway had been completed, so they could commute easily from their new homes into San Francisco. Bourn's house was not destroyed by the earthquake, so he did not hurry to move to the country—that is, not until he purchased the Spring Valley Water Company in 1908. Then he rented the Crocker estate

Sky Farm, adjacent to Crystal Springs Lake, which he had just purchased.

During this time Bourn often took his family to Europe. While on an Atlantic crossing his daughter met Arthur Rose Vincent, an Irishman in the British Foreign Service who was judge advocate in Zanzibar. When Vincent asked Bourn if he could marry Maud, Bourn agreed but forbade her to live in Zanzibar. They were married in 1910 and moved to Ireland, where the Vincent family resided. Bourn went to Ireland several months later to find a suitable house for them and fell in love with Muckross House, which looked out over one of the Lakes of Killarney in County Kerry. (The area, with the Kerry Mountains in the background and the Lakes of Killarney, was very similar to the land of the Spring Valley Water Company.) He bought Muckross House and its surrounding 11,000 acres for Maud and Arthur, and the Bourns became frequent visitors and very much enamored with the beautiful lakeside setting. Bourn now knew he wanted to build his own country estate on the shore of Crystal Springs Lake, but he soon discovered he could not: even though he owned the land and the lake, a law stated that no land supplying the public could return to private use.

Bourn asked his lawyer to find suitable land close to the lake, but it was five years before land became available: 1,800 acres at the lake's southern end. Bourn retained the land from the easternmost creek to the top of the mountain for his private estate and sold the remaining acreage to the Spring Valley Water Company. Cañada Road ran through the property he had kept for himself, so he obtained permission to move the road to the east of his property, where it is today, separated from Filoli by a strip of grassland belonging to the San Francisco Water Department with a permanent easement for the driveway to the Filoli estate.

The origin and meaning of the name of Bourn's estate was a mystery that tantalized his friends for a long time. It was finally discovered that the name comprised the first two letters each of the words *fight, love* and *live,* from a credo in which Bourn placed great stock: "Fight for a just cause, love your fellow man, live a good life."

Once again Bourn turned to his architect friend, Willis Polk, to design his country mansion. Polk drew nineteen different designs for an estate and asked Bourn to select the one he wished for Filoli. Bourn chose the modified English Georgian house, to be constructed with brick. It took nearly two years to build the house from the time the land was cleared in the first week of November 1915. Great pains were taken in siting the house on the oak knoll so as to get the best view and to save the largest of the oak trees. A tall platform was built and moved about on wheels on the knoll to locate the house in the best position. To complete the house in such a short time, a tent city of workers lived in the north field. They were skilled Italian woodworkers and stone masons, single men who had emigrated from Italy to earn money to send to their families at home. When the Bourns moved in at the end of September 1917, the house was nearly totally furnished (the interior of the ballroom was not completed until several years later) and the basic landscaping of the lawns surrounding the house was finished. Toward the end of the work on the house Bourn had a falling-out with Polk and hired Arthur Brown, Jr., to design the eight-car garage known as the Carriage House, the attached chauffeur's quarters, the Garden Pavilion, the gardener's cottage and the greenhouses.

Bourn asked his friend Bruce Porter, who shared Bourn's love of the natural beauty of the California landscape, to design the gardens. Porter was a designer, painter, poet and critic. He had painted the murals in Bourn's house in San Francisco and designed the stained glass windows, and he had previously worked with Polk on several buildings, often doing the interiors. The gardens at Filoli were conceived as a complementary unit integrated with the Transverse Hall of the house. The paths leading out from the hall pass the Sunken Garden and continue through first the Chartres Cathedral Window Garden (designed after one of the stained glass windows at Chartres Cathedral in France) and then the Panel Gardens. Parallel paths to the west cross the Sunken Garden and the Walled Garden to the Yew Allée, which extends to the High Place, with its semicircle of columns. The gardens were designed to enhance the natural landscape and to take advantage of the magnificent view of the mountains to the west and the long, sweeping view to the north. (In Bourn's time, before the second-growth oak trees and madrone trees obscured

Old Cañada Road

the view, the mountains were much more a part of the garden backdrop.)

The gardens were separated by hedges to protect them from the summer winds that sweep down into the valley when the fog bank sits on top of the mountain ridge. The Walled Garden is divided into a series of garden "rooms" within the large enclosure of a brick wall measuring 277 by 167 feet. It is the only area in the gardens with a diagonal accent of terraces rising from the flat area of the garden to its highest area—an ingenious design by Bruce Porter to handle the eleven-foot difference in elevation from the Garden Pavilion to the entrance of the Woodland Garden. The ground could not be made level in the Walled Garden, as Bourn wished, to preserve the large oaks at the western end, so only one of these oaks remains today. In the center of the Walled Garden stands a sundial inscribed with the words "Time Began in a Garden."

In the Dutch Garden within the Walled Garden are two of the rarest trees at Filoli: evergreen New Zealand black beeches (*Nothofagus solandri*) that were brought over for the New Zealand Building at the 1915 Panama-Pacific Exposition. These specimens of *Nothofagus* are considered to be the tallest of their kind growing in the northern hemisphere. Other trees from the 1915 Exposition are the Hinoki false cypress (*Chamaecyparis obtusa*), located near the steps to the path on the West Terrace. These were given to Bourn by the Japanese government at the closing of the Exposition.

Isabella Worn, better known as Bella, supervised the planting of the Filoli gardens. As a young girl Worn had traveled abroad for two years with her mother and sisters and seen the great gardens in Europe. With their imaginative use of flowers, she and her sisters became popular decorators for parties in the San Francisco Bay Area. They abandoned the entire concept of floral displays as stiff bouquets to embrace a more natural, graceful use of flowers. The Bourns had the Worn sisters create lavish themes for their parties, for which the floral decorations created the mood and setting. Bella was a fine garden artist, and Bourn appreciated her clever designs with foliage, fragrance and texture and her keen sense of color. He worked closely with her on the color combinations in the gardens. Bella continued to work in the Filoli gardens with Lurline Roth, the next owner after the Bourns died, and she was working

there three weeks before she died, at age eighty-one.

More than two hundred Irish yews (*Taxus baccata* 'Stricta') were started from cuttings from the yews at Muckross, grown in the greenhouses at the Empire Mine and then planted out. They were dug up and boxed and brought to Filoli as needed for planting in the gardens. The English hollies (*Ilex aquifolium*) and the Chilean myrtle (*Luma apiculata*) were also grown from cuttings from Muckross.

By the spring of 1921 the brickwork in the Walled Garden was completed and the garden was planted. Work on the Panel Gardens began with the planting of dwarf fruit trees along the south-facing wall. Here everything needed for the house was grown: vegetable gardens behind the English laurel hedge (*Prunus laurocerasus*), roses and cut flowers for arranging and espaliered apple and pear trees, which formed a walkway to the High Place. A hedge of the rose of Sharon (*Hibiscus syriacus*) was planted to separate the Rose Garden from the Cutting Gardens, which were broken up by a magnificent seedling copper beech hedge (*Fagus sylvatica* 'Atropunicea') and clipped English holly hedges. Today two neatly trimmed Knot Gardens fill the space between the Rose Garden and the copper beech hedge, and across the path from them is an ornamental vegetable garden bed.

By 1922 the water system for the gardens was completed, piping several springs into a reservoir formed by an earthen dam across the creek high in the mountains. Storage tanks were constructed to hold the water needed for the sixteen acres of gardens, and wells were developed on the lower part of the property. Today the springs feed into new, filtered storage tanks and the wells have been renovated to supply most of the water for the twenty-seven acres under cultivation.

Bourn suffered severe strokes in the summers of 1921 and 1922 that paralyzed his legs and vocal cords and confined him to a wheelchair. Agnes Bourn had to supervise the completion of the ballroom with the help of Arthur Brown, Jr., and the prominent American muralist Ernest Peixotto. In his studio in Paris, Peixotto painted the murals for the ballroom walls, which depict Muckross House and Abbey and the Lakes of Killarney. Peixotto and Maud

Bourn Vincent, also in Paris, helped with selecting the French crystal chandeliers and wall sconces. Agnes Bourn chose what she called the "water green" color for the ballroom. In 1925 the ballroom was ready to host a performance by the great pianist Ignacy Paderewski for the Bourns's friends.

From his wheelchair Bourn maintained an active interest in the development of the gardens. Five differently designed wrought iron gates were made for the Walled Garden. An Irish Yew Allée was planted in front of the espaliered fruit trees framing the walkway to the High Place, where Bourn enjoyed the view through the yews and past the gardens to Crystal Springs Lake. A small part of this view can still be seen in winter, when the valley's deciduous oak trees have lost their leaves.

In 1929, while crossing the Atlantic with her two children en route to California, Maud Bourn Vincent developed pneumonia. She died in New York City and was buried on a knoll in the hills overlooking Filoli. Three years later Agnes Bourn had a stroke and fell into a coma.

That year Bourn had the wrought iron porch completed at the north end of the house so he could continue to watch the sunset over Crystal Springs Lake. He retired completely from the business world, selling the Empire Mine, the San Francisco Gas Company and the Spring Valley Water Company. Muckross House and the surrounding 11,000 acres were presented to the Republic of Ireland as a memorial to Maud, to be called the Bourn-Vincent Memorial Park.

In 1936 both Agnes and William Bourn died, leaving the Filoli estate in trust to their two grandchildren. Both were buried on the knoll overlooking the valley, alongside their daughter, Maud, and their infant son.

THE ROTHS AT FILOLI

Mr. and Mrs. William P. Roth

Filoli was purchased in 1937, complete with furnishings, from the estate of Agnes and William Bourn by William P. and Lurline B. Roth. Mrs. Roth was the daughter of Captain William Matson, founder and president of the Matson Navigation Company and a principal in the establishment of the Honolulu Oil Corporation. Mr. Roth was president and, later, chairman of the board of Matson Navigation Company, until his death at Filoli in 1963.

Mrs. Roth was one of the outstanding horsewomen in the United States; the gaited horses and hackney ponies from her Why Worry Stables in Woodside were champions at shows across the country. She was also an avid and knowledgeable horticulturist who enriched the gardens at Filoli by adding a great variety of flowering shrubs and trees, including hundreds of camellias, rhododendrons, roses and magnolias. Mrs. Roth made Filoli's gardens known worldwide— they were visited by botanical and horticultural societies and many distinguished guests, and she often opened them to benefit charities and other organizations. She wanted the house and gardens preserved for future generations to enjoy, a desire that culminated in her generous endowment and gift of the house and gardens to the National Trust for Historic Preservation in 1975.

In 1958 Mr. and Mrs. Roth were awarded the Garden Club of America's Medal of Merit for making their excellently maintained gardens available to the public. In 1973 Mrs. Roth was awarded the club's Distinguished Service Medal for her achievements as a collector and propagator of noteworthy plants and in recognition of her sustained interest in all areas of horticulture—as a collector of rare orchids, roses, camellias, rhododendrons and magnolias; as a propagator of hundreds of plants for distribution to arboreta; and as a contributor to horticultural knowledge.

When Mrs. Roth took over the gardens at Filoli, she continued with the original plan of color for the annual beds started by Bella Worn. In 1946 she added the swimming pool and, with Bella's help, planned the pool's magnifi-

cent setting. A double row of Irish yews (*Taxus baccata* 'Stricta') was moved from behind the west side of the Yew Allée in the orchard area to form a matching border on the north side of the pool. Behind the newly moved yews was planted an interesting collection of flowering shrubs and trees. Colorful eastern redbud (*Cercis canadensis*), eastern dogwood (*Cornus florida*), beauty bush (*Kolkwitzia amabilis*) and fragrant sweet box (*Sarcococca ruscifolia*) grace the garden in early spring. By late June western azalea (*Rhododendron occidentale*) adds its fragrance, along with glossy abelia (*Abelia* x *grandiflora*). In late summer *Eucryphia* x *intermedia* 'Rostrevor' blooms, with large, white bell-shaped flowers bearing big tufts of yellow stamens; sweet olive osmanthus (*Osmanthus fragrans*) perfumes the air with its tiny, fragrant flowers in early fall. Behind these flowering shrubs and trees are several handsome hollies and new shrubs with attractive foliage for flower arrangements.

Behind the glass-sided Pool Pavilion, constructed as a windscreen for protection from the cool afternoon wind that sweeps into the valley, a handsome yellow-leaved honey locust (*Gleditsia triacanthos* 'Sunburst') was planted. Each spring and fall the leaves turn gold, drawing the eye upward to the grandeur of the Coast Range mountains. To enrich the color scheme and texture further, two Japanese maples, *Acer palmatum* and *Acer palmatum* 'Atropurpurea', were planted, and for soft color, graceful olive trees (*Olea europaea*). To tie the new planting to the Sunken Garden, three more olive trees were added, two in front of the Garden Pavilion and one beside the Sunken Garden's entrance gate. These olive trees and those behind the Pool Pavilion are continually pruned so they are open and airy, allowing their handsome snarled gray limbs to take on a sculptural form. They are kept flat on top and round on the sides, like huge drums; this graceful and unusual way of shaping olive trees was Mrs. Roth's idea. The trees are greatly admired by visitors to the gardens.

Mrs. Roth enlarged the Rose Garden in the Panel Garden, adding some outstanding new roses. She also added extensively to the greenhouse plants and started a superb collection of orchids. Greenhouse plants in bloom were brought into the house for everyone to enjoy, and the Garden Pavilion displayed many of them, as it does today. Behind the brick wall on the west side of the Chartres Cathedral Window Garden she added two deciduous dawn redwoods (*Metasequoia glyptostroboides*). These seedlings came from the first seed collection made in China, in 1948, by Dr. Ralph Chaney, and were given to Mrs. Roth by the Save the Redwoods League.

Mrs. Roth replanted most of the rhododendrons in the Woodland Garden, west of the Walled Garden. When Jock Brydon was director of the Strybing Arboretum in San Francisco, he crossed the rhododendron 'Unknown Warrior' with *R. yakusimanum* and named the cross 'Lurline' in honor of Mrs. Roth. 'Lurline' was planted in the Woodland Garden, which later became too shaded by oaks to allow rhododendrons to bloom properly. Today two beautiful specimens bloom along the path south of the Walled Garden, near the weeping Japanese cherry trees.

Camellias, a favorite of Mrs. Roth, were planted wherever there was room in the gardens and along the drive behind the Carriage House. Japonicas, reticulatas and sasanquas add a great deal of color to the gardens from fall through spring.

On the north side of the front courtyard is one of the loveliest of the many magnolias Mrs. Roth planted, the elegant *Magnolia campbellii* 'Strybing White'. This form is a cultivar of the endangered species *M. campbellii* that was preserved by horticulturists patient enough to wait the twenty years or more the plant requires to bloom. Today, on grafted stock, it comes into bloom earlier. Along the drive in front of the house, Mrs. Roth planted several more white-flowering magnolias and a lovely, fragrant *Michelia doltsopa*, an evergreen relative of the magnolia with numerous creamy white flowers that are borne among the leaves at the same time as the magnolias flower. This plant is not commonly available because of difficulties in propagation and grafting.

Mrs. Roth's love of plants and flowering shrubs is clearly evident in the year-round seasonal color she added to the gardens. Additionally, each year she planted oat hay in the fields surrounding Filoli for her many fine thoroughbred mares and their foals, for the herds of wild deer and for the Canada geese that winter in the fields from November to April.

Her greatest gift, however, was giving Filoli's house and gardens to the National Trust for Historic Preservation in December 1975. In 1982, Mrs. Roth and her family gave the remaining acres of the original Filoli property to Filoli Center in order to preserve Filoli forever in its glorious setting. Mrs. Roth died on September 5, 1985, two days after her ninety-fifth birthday. All of the original Bourn furnishings purchased with Filoli, which she had used at her Hillsborough home since 1975, she willed back to the estate, thus completing her generous gift so that others might continue to enjoy Filoli as she did in the thirty-nine years she lived there.

Black-tailed deer in the north field in springtime

THE SEASONS AT FILOLI

SPRING

Mid-February to Mid-March

Spring at Filoli begins in the middle of February, with the blooming of the *Magnolia campbellii* 'Strybing White' in the Entrance Courtyard, its large flowers resembling white doves perched on the still-leafless branches. The lower petals open flat and the center ones remain tightly upright, leaving an opening just large enough for pollinating insects to enter. Soon the other magnolias in the courtyard burst into bloom. Across the drive and facing the courtyard, white blossoms cover a row of Chinese white magnolias and the air is scented by the white flowers of *Michelia doltsopa*, an evergreen member of the magnolia family. The *Michelia* is slightly more vulnerable to frost and sunburn than are other magnolias, but the large old evergreen oak (*Quercus agrifolia*) across the drive affords it enough protection that it has grown into a fine, tall specimen. One seldom sees *M. doltsopa* in California gardens; it was only recently introduced into horticulture in the Bay Area by the Strybing Arboretum in San Francisco.

At the corner of the Entrance Courtyard, *Magnolia* x *soulangiana* resembles a large pink-and-white cloud, its branches engulfed in blossoms. In the courtyard, the winter-blooming hellebores are still flowering at the feet of the magnolias and the Japanese maples (*Acer palmatum*). Their handsome flowers, in shades from greenish white to deep maroon, are attractive both in flower and with seed pods. Along the brick pathway on the north side of the mansion, the winter daphne (*Daphne odora* 'Marginata') is still blooming, its sweetly fragrant pink flowers delighting all who pass by. White snowdrops (*Leucojum aestivum*) bloom here and there in the bed.

Soon pots of golden daffodils will brighten the steps of the Front Portico to greet visitors. Daffodils, in all their splendid varieties, are a theme of the garden, displayed in dozens of pots around the Garden Pavilion, the Sunken Garden pool and the Sundial; on the slate Dining Room Terrace; in the tiers of the Wedding Place; and in other choice locations. Out in the old orchard on the west side of the Yew Allée in the Panel Garden, an entire slope is covered with thousands of blooming daffodils. Previous years' potted daffodils find a permanent home here.

In the Walled Garden, near the gate to the Woodland Garden, the evergreen *Clematis armandii* drapes its fragrant flowers over the brick wall, adding its perfume to the other sweet scents. The spring-flowering bulbs come into bloom with *Viburnum burkwoodii* as its clusters of pink buds open to very fragrant white flowers. Throughout the garden, the many *Camellia japonica* and *Camellia reticulata* species present their spectacular big flowers. In her love for camellias, Lurline Roth planted so many in Filoli's gardens that there is hardly room for one more.

Mid-March and April

By March, the Japanese weeping cherry trees (*Prunus subhirtella* 'Pendula') are a glorious sight in the Walled Garden, their elegantly cascading flowering branches almost sweeping the ground in some places. In the beds the tulips are in bloom, coming up through bedding plants placed in the fall for color before and after the tulips bloom. The bedding plants most often used are violas (*Viola cornuta* sp.), pink and white forget-me-nots (*Myosotis* 'Carmine King' and *Myosotis* 'White Bouquet'), Chinese forget-me-nots (*Cynoglossum amabile*), gold and orange Siberian wallflowers (*Erysimum hieracifolium*) and pastel shades of columbine (*Aquilegia* sp.).

The first climbing Chinese wisteria (*Wisteria sinensis*) to bloom is on a sun-warmed brick wall in a corner of the Service Courtyard, where it creates a beautiful combination with the yellow-flowered Lady Banks' rose (*Rosa banksiae*). This elegant color scheme is repeated over the entryway to the Administration Office. Other fine specimens of wisteria found in the Service Courtyard area that serves as the Filoli Plant and Tea Shop are *Wisteria floribunda* 'Violaceae Plena', with full clusters of double blue-violet flowers, and *W. venusta*, a white-flowered specimen. Some of the older wisterias trained on the

OPPOSITE: Weeping cherry blossoms (*Prunus subhirtella*)

mansion's walls reach second-floor windows and are a marvelous sight in mid-April as they fill the air with their sweet fragrance. One of the finest views of the Entrance Courtyard occurs then, when the fine old purple Chinese wisteria and the white-starred *Clematis montana* unite at a height of twenty feet on the Italian baroque–style front portico and cascade over the house's main entrance like a floral waterfall. Other fine specimens of Chinese and Japanese wisteria are trained along the balustrade on the mansion's west side. All are beautifully and artfully pruned each year. It is well worth a visit to the estate just to see one of the finest collections of wisteria on the West Coast in bloom.

Filoli's many rhododendron species, including the popular large-flowered types as well as the small-flowered evergreen azaleas, are found extensively throughout the Woodland and Walled Gardens. Their blooming season is from late March through May. One especially lovely rhododendron is 'Lurline', named for Mrs. Roth. It is a cross of *R. yakusimanum* and *R.* 'Unknown Warrior' made at the Strybing Arboretum and given to Mrs. Roth in appreciation of her love for rhododendrons.

Although the Woodland Garden is primarily the home of many exquisite camellia and rhododendron species and varieties, it also possesses some fine specimens of white and pink eastern dogwood, *Cornus florida* and *Cornus florida* 'Rubra', which come into full bloom during the flowering season of the camellias and rhododendrons. Chinese dogwood (*C. kousa*), also located in the Woodland Garden, blooms later in June and July, bearing flowers that stand above its leaves along the tops of its branches.

At the end of the vista from the Sunken Garden, behind the Pool Pavilion, the brilliant yellow new leaves of the honey locust tree (*Gleditsia triacanthos* 'Sunburst') draw the eye upward to a magnificent view of the Coast Range mountains. To the left, at the end of the Bowling Green, the Camperdown elms (*Ulmus glabra* 'Camperdownii') have clothed their branches in clusters of chartreuse seed pods that from a distance look like flowering petals. The Camperdown elms are a spectacular sight at this time of year. Their twisted and gnarled branches bear clusters of seed pods followed by enormous dark green leaves that drape nearly to the ground, creating a tent

effect. In any season, these specimens are a glorious sight.

In the Walled Garden the pink-flowering crab apple trees (*Malus* sp.) strike a brilliant contrast with the Kurume azalea cultivars—the brilliant red 'Ward's Ruby' and the cerise 'Hinodegiri'—blooming beneath them. The hawthorn trees (*Crataegus phaenopyrum*) near the gate to the Panel Garden are carefully pruned and trained to look like white-flowering umbrellas when in bloom.

Another lovely view at this time of year is found on entering the Panel Garden and looking up through the four tiers of the Yew Allée to the High Place, with its semicircle of stone pillars. (The pillars were used as ballast in old sailing ships that were deserted by crews in search of gold. Both the pillars and the ships' anchor chains were made available to anyone.) A lawn runs up the middle of the Allée and is edged on both sides by evergreen candytuft (*Iberis sempervirens*), whose masses of white flowers resemble white lace against the dark green of the Irish yew columns (*Taxus baccata* 'Stricta'). The effect is heightened by a mass of pink tulip pots at the entrance to the Allée, at elevation changes of each of the tiers and at the High Place itself. The stone pillars at the High Place are draped with wisteria blossoms, and a huge yew hedge stands behind them.

A lovely shrub that blooms in April is the pearl bush (*Exochorda racemosa*). Two stand on either side of the brick steps in the Upper Panel Garden leading to the Yew Allée. Their delicate white flowers open from buds that truly resemble tiny pearls. In the Chartres Cathedral Window Garden there is a double form of the pearl bush (*Exochorda* x *macrantha* 'The Bride').

Other bedding plants used throughout the garden in April are foxgloves, sweet williams and violas.

May and June

Roses are abloom everywhere in the gardens by Mother's Day. The Rose Garden is a solid mass of color, from the deep red, sweet-scented *Rosa* 'Mr. Lincoln' to the very pale white *R.* 'Iceberg'. Superb climbing specimens trained against the

View of the Garden Pavilion from the South Terrace lawn, with Chinese wisteria (*Wisteria sinensis*)

27

warm south-facing walls of the Panel Garden include some of the finest single-flowered varieties, such as the deep red *R.* 'Altissimo' and the light pink *R.* 'Kathleen'. 'Kathleen' has been trained to twine about the sides of Bourn Gate up to the feet of the eagles perched there so that the eagles appear to be gazing out from an eyrie of roses. The collection of roses in the Rose Garden section of the Panel Gardens numbers in the hundreds, consisting of the modern rose types—hybrid teas, floribundas, polyanthas and miniature roses in both bush and tree form. A selection of tree roses forms an integral part of the Chartres Cathedral Window Garden in the Walled Garden area. A separate, smaller area of old-fashioned roses is maintained west of the mansion near the Northwest Terrace Lawn. Here one can see the earliest rose bushes, such as the China rose (*R. chinensis*), the damask rose (*R. damascena*), the cabbage rose (*R. centifolia*), the York rose (*R. alba*), the French rose (*R. gallica*) and many others, all leading to the development of the modern hybrid tea roses. Many of the old-fashioned roses possess unique fragrances not commonly found in modern roses.

In the upper beds of the Panel Gardens the glorious tree peonies (*Paeonia* hybrids) are sensational in April and May. Most of the tree peonies were a gift from Toichi Domoto, a well-known Bay Area nurseryman and hybridizer who had an outstanding collection of them. Most bear gigantic flowers (up to twelve inches in diameter) and come in beautiful shades from pure white through pale creams, yellows and pinks to red. The tree peony needs less winter chill to bloom than does its herbaceous relative. Filoli's location in an inland coastal valley provides enough chilling for the tree peonies to bloom beautifully, and the herbaceous peonies, planted in the coldest area of the gardens, also bloom spectacularly in May.

In May, many iris hybrids, a gift from the West Bay Iris Society, bloom in the long Perennial Border on the west side of the Lower Lawn Terrace, creating an interesting and colorful show of the Society's best cultivars. The bearded iris named for Filoli, *Iris* 'Filoli', blooms in the bed by the low brick wall in the Service Courtyard. In the Panel Garden along both sides of the lower path is an entire border of white bearded iris several hundred feet long.

The 300-foot-long Perennial Border, a gift of the Hillsborough Garden Club, comes into bloom in late spring and blooms throughout the summer months. In late spring it is a panorama of catmint (*Nepeta* x *faassenii*); pale yellow yarrow (*Achillea* 'Moonshine'); blue speedwell (*Veronica incana*); the lavender-blue balloon flower, *Platycodon grandiflorus,* whose flower buds look like tiny balloons before they open; deep blue sages (*Salvia* x *superba* 'May Night', *S. guaranitica* and the tall *S. uliginosa*); yellow hot poker (*Kniphofia uvaria* 'Butterpat'); and yellow-flowered Jerusalem sage (*Phlomis fruticosa*). Garden penstemon (*Penstemon gloxinoides*) and *Rosa* 'Ballerina' add a touch of pink to the design, and gray foliage plants soften the edges of the border. *Tanacetum haradjanii,* with its flat, feathery, finely cut leaves resembling miniature ostrich plumes; lamb's ears (*Stachys byzantia*), whose soft, woolly leaves are delightful to feel; and *Artemisia* 'Powis Castle', with its delicate, airy form, all serve this function nicely. Two purple-leaved smoke trees (*Cotinus coggygria* 'Royal Purple') add a distinctive reddish purple to the border's overall design. The textures, sizes, shapes and colors in this unique border create an inspiring example of what can be done in California with drought-tolerant perennials. Running the entire length of the border to the east is a grand English laurel hedge (*Prunus laurocerasus*). Its glossy deep green leaves provide an excellent backdrop for the subtle colors of the border.

The Knot Gardens, a gift of the Woodside-Atherton Garden Club, are very colorful when the dwarf English lavender hedges (*Lavandula angustifolia* 'Hidcote') are in bloom, contrasting with the deep green of the germander hedges (*Teucrium chamaedrys*) and the red of the Japanese barberry (*Berberis thunbergii* 'Crimson Pigmy'). A tall copper beech hedge (*Fagus sylvatica* 'Atropunicea') provides a rich bronze backdrop for the southern Knot Garden. The northern Knot Garden (each has a different design) contrasts the gray-green leaves of lavender cotton (*Santolina chamaecyparissus* 'Nana') with the dark green of germander and the red of Japanese barberry. Clipped rounded balls of dwarf myrtle (*Myrtus communis* 'Microphylla') accent the center and corners of the bed. In June, when the Knot Gardens are at their best and the Perennial Border and Rose Garden are blooming in full splendor, a visit to the Panel Gardens is a rewarding experience.

Eagle atop Bourn Gate, in a nest of climbing roses (*Rosa* 'Kathleen')

29

Beyond the Knot Gardens and to the west is the ornamental vegetable garden, newly designed by garden superintendent Lucy Tolmach. Ornamental vegetable gardens are of great interest today, combining edible vegetables with formal borders of low hedges or flowers. For a long period they were not fashionable, but their popularity is returning. The oldest known such garden is located at Villandry in France, near Tours. Rosemary Verey, a well-known English horticulturist and garden writer, applied her expert hand and designed an outstanding ornamental vegetable garden at Barnsley House, her home in England. Her project's success has helped increase public awareness of the beauty and practicality of such gardens. At Filoli, a lavender hedge surrounds the kitchen garden on three sides. The path leading into the garden has a circular bed in the center planted with edible flowers, herbs and greens. A low hedge of germander encloses this bed as well as the outer borders of the four beds, two on each side of the center bed. In the back, a carved redwood bench invites visitors to rest and admire the overall effect of this cheerful garden with vegetables contrasting in both texture and color. Miniature knot gardens, replicas of the Knot Gardens across the path, stand at each side of the entrance to the kitchen garden. Created for a flower show at Gump's in San Francisco in 1992, they are kept beautifully trimmed by one of Filoli's dedicated garden volunteers.

SUMMER

By the end of May, all the annual flower beds have been replanted so that by late June a whole new floral display will be ready for the summer visitors. All the spring-flowering plants, including the tulips, are removed and composted. A typical example is the replanting of the Sunken Garden from tulips, violas, columbines and Chinese forget-me-nots to pink petunias, white annual salvias and summer phlox. Many combinations are possible; emphasis is placed on themes of blue, white and pink. Begonias, zinnias, geraniums, delphiniums, salvias, impatiens, summer phlox, verbenas, cosmos and several other annuals are selected either individually or in combination to create col-

orful and pleasing effects throughout the garden. Once planted, the summer beds will remain in bloom until October, when they will be replanted once again for spring.

A startling sight and one always pleasing to the visitor in late summer is the beautiful sky blue morning glory *Ipomoea* 'Heavenly Blue' along the path in the Upper Panel Garden. Its vines completely cover the wire cages on either side of the path with their beautiful yellow-throated blue flowers. Vines put on a summer show in other areas as well. The royal purple flowers of *Clematis jackmanii* grace the balustrade of the Sunken Garden, along with the orange-red trumpet flowers of *Campsis grandiflora*.

By August the cashmere bouquet (*Clerodendrum bungei*) is in bloom in the Entrance Courtyard, under the Japanese maples and the magnolias on the Ballroom side. Its large clusters of rosy pink flowers are fragrant and long lasting. The creamy white flowers of the large evergreen southern magnolia (*Magnolia grandiflora*) on the front lawn near the entrance to the Service Courtyard bloom over a long period among shiny, dark green leaves. Behind the magnolia, next to the brick wall, the tall flower spikes of *Acanthus mollis* 'Latifolius' add a classical touch to the formal landscape.

In the beds on the west side of the house, dwarf pomegranates (*Punica granatum* 'Nana') show their orange-red tubular flowers, followed shortly by their lovely fruit. These foundation bed plants have been painstakingly pruned so that their flowers and fruit are displayed as individual bouquets on the ends of their branches. The lavender flowers of the shrub verbena *Lantana montevidensis* bloom in several beds. In shady areas of the garden are seen the large flower heads of hydrangeas (*Hydrangea macrophylla*) in shades of deep rose and blue. In late August the Chilean myrtle (*Luma apiculata*), a tree from the southern hemisphere, is covered with masses of white flowers. The lovely smooth, cinnamon-colored bark of these outstanding trees exfoliates in patches, leaving temporary greenish-white areas.

Along the paths in the Woodland Garden and in other shady areas, an exquisite little flower comes into bloom during the late summer months—the tiny hardy cyclamen (*Cyclamen hederifolium*). It is a delicate flower in shades of white or rose pink on three- to four-inch stems with heart-shaped leaves marbled silver and white.

Just as in springtime, a great many flowering pots are placed in the garden to enhance the beauty of the summer scene. One particularly interesting, easy-to-maintain and very long lasting potted display is a combination of scented, ivy-leaved and variegated geraniums. This arrangement has the look of a Victorian bouquet and enjoys the added benefit of requiring comparatively little water.

The summer season at Filoli has its own unique beauty, characterized by splashes of color in the annual beds combined with special perennial displays of hydrangeas, pomegranates, cyclamens and roses, all surrounded by the many greens and grays of magnificent oaks, cedars, elms, olives, hornbeams, hollies, laurels and the like. The changes that occur between late June and October are perhaps less dramatic than the spectacular transformation of the garden into a magical floral kingdom in the spring months, but the elegant, graceful and refined nature of the formal display garden is fully revealed in summer.

FALL

The first sign of fall appears in the garden in late October, when the Virginia creeper (*Parthenocissus quinquefolia*) on the sunny brick wall on the east side of the Chartres Cathedral Window Garden turns a brilliant scarlet red. Next, the pale green needles of the dawn redwood (*Metasequoia glyptostroboides*) turn a soft bronze, spreading a warm glow over the garden. By the third week in November the color change is in full swing, and it remains so through the first week of December.

The Camperdown elm, so elegant and graceful in spring and so grand in summer, adds another dimension of wonder in the fall. Its leaves gradually change from dark green to rich gold; this color change displayed on its weeping branches creates the effect of a shimmering golden waterfall. Nearby, along the brick wall that separates the Bowling Green from the Woodland Garden, is a climbing hydrangea (*Hydrangea anomala petiolaris*). During the summer

months it accents the wall with its graceful shape and green leaves, but its real glory comes in the fall, when its leaves change to a vibrant, green-veined gold. It stands out even more during this season because the London plane trees (*Platanus* x *acerifolia*) have been pollarded, so it is no longer hidden in their shade. Rising directly above the climbing hydrangea on the Woodland Garden side is a towering Japanese maple whose delicate, tiny palm-shaped leaves turn a rich red. When the leaves fall, they carpet the path and the steps to the Tennis Court with a mantle of regal color. Behind and rising above the Camperdown elms is another magnificent Japanese maple, this one with orange leaves. It is a glorious sight when all of these neighboring trees display their fall beauty.

Many other excellent specimens of Japanese maple are located in shady sections of the gardens, each contributing a unique hue to the fall scene. All of Filoli's Japanese maples came from the historic Domoto Nursery. Established in 1897 by Toichi Domoto's father, who introduced the Kurume azalea at the 1915 Panama-Pacific Exposition in San Francisco, the Domoto Nursery continues to provide specimens for the gardens from its special collections of maples, peonies, Japanes iris and other plants.

One of the most splendid sights in the gardens occurs when the fan-shaped leaves of the ginkgo trees (*Ginkgo biloba*) turn to a pure yellow-gold and fall, laying a golden carpet on the paths and covering the tops of the boxwood hedges. When this spectacle is combined with the colors of the nearby hawthorn tree—in itself a rare fall treat, with the many shades of red in its leaves and its branches covered with thousands of scarlet berries—the beauty of the scene is dramatic. Adding to the general atmosphere in this part of the garden are two grand American hornbeam trees (*Carpinus caroliniana*). The gold of their leaves is more subtle than that of the ginkgoes, but they are beautiful in their own right.

Many other lovely fall colors greet the eye as one walks through the garden at this time of year. The weeping cherries turn a fine gold; wisterias with their brown pods turn a rich bronze; the Boston ivy and Virginia creeper clinging to the walls display many shades of red; and the hollies, with their dark red berries against green leaves, present a pleasing sight. All this and more form

Dressing room window of the Bath House surrounded by colorful leaves of variegated Virginia creeper (*Parthenocissus henryana*)

one of the most colorful autumn landscapes imaginable.

By the second week of December, most of the fall color has disappeared and the garden rests for a brief period. With the leaves of the deciduous trees gone and the beds planted with flowers that will bloom in the spring, a much more basic vision of the garden appears. This is a good time of year to see how the garden's architecture was laid out when the estate was established. Because Filoli is one of the last surviving examples from the golden age of American gardens, every effort is made by its staff of professional gardeners, student interns and dedicated volunteers to preserve the gardens as they were created by the Bourns and the Roths.

33

ABOVE: The daffodil field in the Panel Garden in early spring, with the mansion in the background

OPPOSITE: View of the Clock Tower and Garden Pavilion from the Dining Room Terrace, with potted daffodils surrounding a red oak

35

East-facing view of the Sunken Garden pool,
with a display of potted daffodils

View of the Garden Pavilion across the Sunken Garden, with potted daffodils

THE GARDEN PHOTOGRAPHS

ABOVE: Interior of the Garden Pavilion, with various indoor plants

OPPOSITE: The Garden Pavilion lawn, with pool in the foreground and copper font with camellias in the background

Bourn Gate as viewed facing north from the Panel Garden, with two American hornbeam trees (*Carpinus caroliniana*)

The Sundial in early spring, prior to the spring floral display

ABOVE: The Wedding Place font and Festina Lente Gate, with evergreen clematis (*Clematis armandii*)

OPPOSITE: Terraces of the Wedding Place, with magnolia (*Magnolia* x *soulangiana* 'Rustica Rubra') on the right, weeping cherry (*Prunus subhirtella*) on the left and a fifteenth-century font in the background

43

Gate opening into the Woodland Garden from the Panel Garden, with evergreen clematis (*Clematis armandii*) climbing on the wall

Path leading from the Woodland Garden to the steps of the Tennis Court, with camellia (*Camellia reticulata*) in the foreground

ABOVE: South-facing view of the Lower Lawn Terrace on a foggy morning, with Irish yew (*Taxus baccata* 'Stricta')

OPPOSITE: Dawson magnolia in the mansion's courtyard on a foggy morning, framed by coast live oak (*Quercus agrifolia*)

THE GARDEN PHOTOGRAPHS

The Bourn Door to the Gift Shop, with *Viburnum* x *burkwoodii* on the right

Eagle atop Bourn Gate, in front of Yulan magnolia (*Magnolia denudata*)

ABOVE: West-facing view of Numbered Beds in the Walled Garden planted with blue and white anemones (*Anemone blanda*) and white tulips (*Tulipa* hybrids), with camellia on the left and weeping cherry tree on the right

OPPOSITE: Pink and white primroses in the Chartres Cathedral Window Garden, facing south

The Sundial, with a view through Bourn Gate toward the High Place, with white and yellow potted daffodils

THE GARDENS AT FILOLI

The Dutch Garden, with two giant New Zealand beech trees (*Nothofagus solandri*) to the right and pink and white camellias in the background

53

ABOVE: Flowering dogwoods (*Cornus florida*) in the Woodland Garden

OPPOSITE: The Garden Pavilion as seen through the branches of a weeping cherry tree (*Prunus subhirtella*)

THE GARDEN PHOTOGRAPHS

Chinese wisteria (*Wisteria sinensis*) trained on the back wall of the mansion

Rear entrance to the mansion, with potted daffodils on the steps, bedded tulips in front of boxwood hedges (*Buxus sempervirens*)
and clematis (*Clematis montana* 'Rubra') climbing the wall

ABOVE: Tulips in the Cut Flower Beds in the Panel Garden, in front of a copper beech hedge (*Fagus sylvatica*)

OPPOSITE: View of the mansion across the Sunken Garden, with Siberian wallflowers (*Erysimum* sp.) and white tulips in beds

The Sundial in its spring glory, with bedded pink tulips in front of weeping cherries (*Prunus subhirtella*) and showy crab apple (*Malus floribunda*)

Close-up view of the Sundial, with weeping cherries and white Japanese wisteria (*Wisteria floribunda* 'Longissima Alba')

THIS PAGE: Weeping cherry tree (*Prunus subhirtella*) in
the Panel Garden

OPPOSITE: Weeping cherry tree (*Prunus subhirtella*)
and tulips (*Tulipa* hybrids) in the Walled Garden

View through Bourn Gate to the High Place, with crisp boxwood hedges (*Buxus sempervirens*) in the foreground and American hornbeam trees (*Carpinus caroliniana*) south of the gate

View of the Clock Tower across the Sunken Garden pool, with waterlilies (*Nymphaea* hybrids)
and cattails (*Typha latifolia*) in the pool and potted tulips in the foreground

65

Filoli Gate decked with wisteria

Chinese wisteria (*Wisteria sinensis*) and eastern redbud
(*Cercis canadensis*) as viewed from the Dining Room Terrace

Close-up view of wisteria on Filoli Gate

View to the west across the Lower Balustrade Bed, with golden honey locust (*Gleditsia triacanthos* 'Sunburst') in the background and Chinese wisteria (*Wisteria sinensis*) in the foreground

69

ABOVE: Chinese wisteria (*Wisteria sinensis*) and Lady Banks' rose (*Rosa banksiae*) trained on the entrance to the Administrative Offices

OPPOSITE: View in the Walled Garden looking toward Bourn Gate, with white Japanese wisteria (*Wisteria floribunda*) and Ward's ruby azaleas (*Rhododendron* 'Ward's Ruby')

THE GARDEN PHOTOGRAPHS

North-facing view of the Sundial in spring, with the mansion in the background

North-facing view of the Sundial, with Ward's ruby azaleas (*Rhododendron* 'Ward's Ruby') in the foreground, pink tulips in beds and weeping cherries in the background, all framed from above by the branches of a ginkgo tree (*Ginkgo biloba*)

73

ABOVE: A large bed of pink and cream-colored peonies (*Paeonia lactiflora*) in the Cut Flower Beds in the Panel Garden, with the High Place in the background

OPPOSITE: Camperdown elm (*Ulmus glabra* 'Camperdownii') at the west end of the Bowling Green

THE GARDEN PHOTOGRAPHS

South-facing view of the Chartres Cathedral Window Garden, with tree roses (*Rosa* hybrid) and purple rockcress (*Aubrieta deltoidea*)

The Sunken Garden, as viewed looking east toward the Clock Tower and the Garden Pavilion, with columbines (*Aquilegia* hybrids),
Chinese forget-me-nots (*Cynoglossum amabile*) and Korean chrysanthemums (*Chrysanthemum paludosum*)

ABOVE: North-facing view of the Perennial Border in the Panel Garden. Shrubs include smoke tree (*Cotinus coggygria*), snowball bush (*Viburnum opulus*), bridal wreath (*Spiraea* x *vanhouttei*) and ballerina rose (*Rosa* 'Ballerina'); perennials include wormwood (*Artemisia* 'Powis Castle'), catmint (*Nepeta* x *faassenii*), balloon flower (*Platycodon grandiflorus*), bee blossom (*Gaura lindheimeri*), woolly lamb's ear (*Stachys byzantia*) and bog sage (*Salvia uliginosa*)

OPPOSITE: View from the Wedding Place toward the Garden Pavilion, with beds of sweet william (*Dianthus barbatus*) and Chinese forget-me-not (*Cynoglossum amabile*)

Overview of the Knot Garden, looking south, with lavender cotton (*Santolina chamaecyparissus* 'Nana'), germander (*Teucrium chamaedrys*), Japanese barberry (*Berberis thunbergii* 'Crimson Pigmy'), dwarf English lavender (*Lavandula angustifolia* 'Hidcote') and dwarf myrtle (*Myrtus communis* 'Microphylla')

Detail of the Knot Garden

THIS PAGE: View of the Sundial through Filoli Gate

OPPOSITE: Roses in front of the Panel Garden Gate

THE GARDEN PHOTOGRAPHS

ABOVE: Closer view of the Sundial, showing beds of white and blue salvia (*Salvia farinacea*), pink and white annual phlox (*Phlox drummondii*) and blue, purple and white lobelia (*Lobelia erinus*)

OPPOSITE: Southwest-facing view of the Sundial in summer

ABOVE: The High Place, facing south, with London plane trees (*Platanus* x *acerifolia*) and tall Irish yew (*Taxus baccata* 'Stricta')

OPPOSITE: The Wedding Place in summer

ABOVE: View of the Dutch Garden, with beds of impatiens

OPPOSITE: The Pool and Pool Pavilion, with potted geraniums (*Pelargonium* sp.) at poolside

95

ABOVE: Display of summer annuals in the Cutting Garden

OPPOSITE: Cut flower cages in the Panel Garden planted with delphiniums (*Delphinium elatum*)

99

The Lower Balustrade Bed to the north of the Sunken Garden, planted with purple petunias (*Petunia* hybrids),
yellow and cream-colored zinnias (*Zinnia elegans*) and purple verbena (*Verbena* hybrids); orange trumpet vines (*Campsis radicans*)
and purple clematis (*Clematis jackmanii*) grow on the wall

THE GARDENS AT FILOLI

The Upper Balustrade Bed near the mansion, planted with pink geraniums (*Pelargonium hortorum*) and purple clematis (*Clematis jackmanii*)

101

ABOVE: West-facing view of the Bowling Green, with pollarded London plane trees (*Platanus* x *acerifolia*) on the left, columns of Irish yew trees (*Taxus baccata* 'Stricta') on the right and golden Camperdown elm (*Ulmus glabra* 'Camperdownii') in the center

OPPOSITE: View of the Bowling Green facing east toward the Garden Pavilion, with London plane trees on the right and columns of Irish yew trees on the left

Fall vista of the road bordering the east side of the garden

THE GARDENS AT FILOLI

View of the Sundial through Filoli Gate in the fall

ABOVE: The Sundial in early morning light

OPPOSITE: Fall view across the Sundial to the Wedding Place pool

North-facing view of the Garden Pavilion and pool, with ginkgo (*Ginkgo biloba*) leaves carpeting the lawn and covering the hedge

Hedges near the Sundial covered with ginkgo leaves

ABOVE: Partial view of the Wedding Place font, with red leaves of Japanese maple (*Acer palmatum*) and golden leaves of Japanese snowbell (*Styrax japonica*)

OPPOSITE: Japanese snowbells above the Wedding Place font

111

Entrance to the Woodland Garden from the Bowling Green,
with leaves of climbing hydrangea (*Hydrangea anomala petiolaris*) cascading over an old bench

Entrance to the Woodland Garden from the Panel Garden, with Japanese maples (*Acer palmatum*)
and hydrangeas (*Hydrangea macrophylla*) providing fall color

113

ABOVE: Numbered Beds in the Walled Garden covered with leaves of ginkgo (*Ginkgo biloba*)

OPPOSITE: Steps leading to the Tennis Courts, carpeted with leaves of Japanese maple (*Acer palmatum*)

Newly pollarded London plane trees (*Platanus* x *acerifolia*)
on the Bowling Green, with golden climbing hydrangea
(*Hydrangea anomala petiolaris*) growing on the wall
and Japanese maple (*Acer palmatum*) above

View to the west from the Pool Pavilion, with leafless honey locust (*Gleditsia triacanthos* 'Sunburst') in the foreground and Japanese maples (*Acer palmatum*) in the background

117

ABOVE: Rust-colored cattails (*Typha latifolia*) in the Sunken Garden, with bush germander (*Teucrium fructicans*) to the left and right

OPPOSITE: Boston ivy (*Parthenocissus tricuspidata*) growing on the balustrade behind the mansion

119

View of Bourn Gate looking toward the High Place, with 'Washington Thorn' hawthorn trees (*Crataegus phaenopyrum*) covered with red berries in the foreground and golden leaves of American hornbeam (*Carpinus caroliniana*) carpeting the path

The eagles atop Bourn Gate, surrounded by fall color

121

THIS PAGE: Golden Japanese maple (*Acer palmatum*) viewed through the entrance gate to the Sunken Garden area

OPPOSITE: View through pollarded London plane trees (*Platanus* x *acerifolia*) to orange crape myrtle (*Lagerstroemia indica*) and golden American hornbeam (*Carpinus caroliniana*)

Fall color in the Walled Garden

Chinese wisteria (*Wisteria sinensis*) growing on a balustrade near the mansion, with a newly shaped olive tree (*Olea europaea*) in the background

125

ABOVE: Frost in the Rose Garden, with a persimmon tree (*Diospyros kaki*) in the background

OPPOSITE: Frost covering the Knot Garden

A frost-covered Camperdown elm (*Ulmus glabra* 'Camperdownii')